W9-BLR-257

*Dear* _____,

*I'm praying for you, Mom, that*

_____

_____

_____

_____

_____

_____

_____

_____

_____

_____

_____

_____

*Love,*

_____

*I'm Praying for You, Mom*

# I'm Praying for You, Mom

## Prayers and Inspiration for All You Encounter in Life

LARRY KEEFAUVER

**Andrews McMeel
Publishing**

Kansas City

I dedicate this book to the special mothers
in my life—Sara and Doris.

*I'm Praying for You, Mom* copyright © 2002 by Larry Keefauver.
All rights reserved. Printed in Hong Kong. No part of this book
may be used or reproduced in any manner whatsoever without
written permission except in the case of reprints in the context
of reviews. For information, write Andrews McMeel Publishing,
an Andrews McMeel Universal company, 4520 Main Street,
Kansas City, Missouri 64111.

02 03 04 05 06 KWF 10 9 8 7 6 5 4 3 2 1

ISBN: 0-7407-2704-4

Library of Congress Control Number: 2002102325

Book design by Holly Camerlinck

*I'm Praying for You, Mom*

# *M*om, I'm praying for you.

Today, right now, this very moment, you are in my thoughts and prayers. I'm not praying out of duty but out of love for you.

Not only did you bring me into this world, you nurtured and cared for me when I was helpless and powerless.

You did for me what I could not do for myself in those formative years of infancy and childhood.

How thankful I am for you! So my daily prayer for you is . . .

*God, bless and protect, care and provide*
*for my mom.*
*In her rising up and lying down,*
*In her going out and coming in,*
*In her laughter and tears,*
*In her work and her leisure,*
*Lord, be her constant companion.*
*Hold her hand through every*
*tough spot today,*
*So that she may feel my touch and yours,*
*My love and yours,*
*My care and yours. Amen.*

This day is a day like no other. It's filled with possibilities and opportunities. Today overflows with God's presence and my love for you. I may not be able physically to see or talk with you today, but I will connect with you spiritually through prayer. I am praying for your health and your well-being.

Mom, today I am declaring shalom over all you are, all you do, and all you will encounter. Shalom speaks of peace, well-being, prosperity, health, wholeness, and living in harmony with God and those around you.

*May shalom fill your thoughts,*
*conversations,*
*relationships,*
*and feelings this day.*
*Mom, I love you!*

# Always There

God could not be everywhere
and therefore
He made mothers.

*Jewish Proverb*

## God, I thank you that Mom . . .

*Was always there.*

*As a child, it seemed to me that Mom
was a lot like you, God.
Mom seemed to be everywhere.*

*At least, she was always there when I
needed her . . .
Especially when I hurt, was tired, or
simply needed a snack.*

*God, help me now to be there for Mom,
whenever and wherever
she needs me to be.
Amen.*

# Mother's Prayers

I remember my mother's prayers
and they have always followed me.
They have clung to me all my life.

*Abraham Lincoln*

## Now, I'm praying for you, Mom.

*Now, turnabout is fair play.*
*Lord, help Mom to realize that even as*
*she prayed for me,*
*now, I pray for her.*

*Lord, help me remember daily all*
*the prayers Mom prayed for me.*
*Empower me to pray for my children the*
*same way Mom prayed for me.*

*Fill me with the strength and*
*determination to pray for Mom even*
*when I am weak and forgetful.*
*Amen.*

# Mother's Devotion

This is the reason why mothers are more
devoted to their children than fathers:
*It is that they suffer more in giving them birth
and are more certain that they are
their own.*

*Aristotle*

# I praise you, God . . .

*For my mother's devotion.*
*I praise God for Mom's*
*faith in me . . .*
*patience in listening to me . . .*
*encouragement when I fail . . .*
*tears of pride when I made it!*

*God, I rejoice in a mother who*
*changed my diapers,*
*wiped my nose,*
*dried my tears,*
*bandaged my hurts,*
*and kissed my forehead.*
*Amen.*

#  A Mother's Love

A father may turn his back on his child;
brothers and sisters may become inveterate enemies;
husbands may desert their wives and wives their husbands.
But a mother's love endures through all;
in good repute, in bad repute,
in the face of the world's condemnation,
a mother still loves on, and still hopes that her child
may turn from his evil ways, and repent;
still she remembers the infant smiles
that once filled her bosom with rapture,
the merry laugh, the joyful shout of his childhood,
the opening promise of his youth;
and she can never be brought to think him all unworthy.

*Washington Irving*

*God, fill Mom with love.*

*This day,*
*in every way,*
*whatever Mom may do or say,*
*lace her words with love,*
*soothe her hurts with love,*
*permeate her thoughts with love,*
*saturate her feelings with love—*
*love for you,*
*love for herself,*
*and love for others.*

*God, I thank you for my mom's love.*
*Amen.*

# $\mathscr{A}$ Mother's Work

By and large, mothers and housewives
are the only workers
who do not have regular time off.
They are the great vacationless class.

*Anne Morrow Lindbergh*

*As you work, I'm praying for you . . .*

*To find fulfillment in every task.*
*May your duties be delights,*
*your chores be joys,*
*your frustrations melt away,*
*your irritations create pearls,*
*your burdens be light,*
*your tears be wiped away*
*by the touch of God.*
*Amen.*

15

# Mother Throughout Life

When you're a child
she walks before you,
To set an example.

When you're a teenager
she walks behind you
To be there should you need her.

When you're an adult she walks beside
you so that as two friends
you can enjoy life together.

*Author Unknown*

*You are my example.*

*I thank you, Lord,*
*for the example of my mother.*

*I thank you, Lord,*
*that she has been behind me*
*to catch me when I fall.*

*I thank you, Lord,*
*that we can talk,*
*friend to friend.*
*Amen.*

# Busy Moms

I leap out of bed.
Baby is fed.
I throw on my clothes.
I wipe the kid's nose.
I pull out some cash.
I step on the gas.
Baby's secured in the cart.
I march through the mart.

I mustn't dawdle.
I feed baby his bottle.
I finish one chore.
I leave the store.
I look at my list.
I give baby a kiss.
I could fall to the floor, but . . .
There's more, more, more!

*B. C. Latin*

*Because you're busy . . .*

*I'm praying for you, Mom.*
*As you rush about, I pray for safety.*
*When you tire, I pray for rest.*
*When others hassle you,*
*I pray for quiet moments in your day*
*Filled with good memories and precious images*
*of family and friends.*

*God, be the still small voice in my*
*mom's day filling her silence with quiet assurance and*
*affirming words.*
*Amen.*

# You're My Friend

Is my mother my friend?
I would have to say,
first of all she is my Mother,
with a capital "M";
she's something sacred to me.
I love her dearly. . . .
Yes, she is also a good friend,
someone I can talk openly to if I want to.

*Sophia Loren*

## I'm praying for you, friend.

Lord, you know I need a friend.
One who listens instead of lectures.
One who gives instead of takes.
One who cares instead of critiques.
One who's there for me.

I beseech you, O Lord,
To give Mom friends
as dear to her
as she is to me.
Amen.

# $\mathcal{Y}$our Best for Me

I looked on child rearing not only as a
work of love and duty but as a
profession that was fully as interesting
and challenging as any honorable
profession in the world and one that
demanded the best I could bring to it.

*Rose Kennedy*

*Mom, you did your best.*

*Lord, I know that Mom didn't*
*know all about raising me,*
*but for giving her best*
*even when she was tired or sick,*
*I am so thankful.*
*Lord, forgive me for the times I*
*rebelled, resisted, and refused*
*to receive your best for me*
*through Mom.*
*Amen.*

# *M*om, I Owe You

It seems to me that my mother was the
most splendid woman I ever knew. . . .
I have met a lot of people knocking
around the world since,
but I have never met a more
thoroughly refined woman
than my mother.
If I have amounted to anything,
it will be due to her.

*Charles Chaplin*

# I'm in debt to you, Mom.

Lord, you know I hate owing
anything to anybody.

But really, God, I'm in debt to Mom
for so much.

Help me to pay my debt to her
By loving her, my family, and others
with the depth of love she gave to me.
Enable me to nurture others
the way she nurtured me.
And grant me, Lord,
the ability to use
the wisdom she taught me
every step of my way.
Amen.

# $\mathcal{M}$y Hurt and Worries

Mother—
that was the bank
where we deposited
our hurts and worries.

*T. DeWitt Talmage*

*When you hurt, Mom . . .*

*I pray that you will deposit
your pain into my caring,
your hurt into my praying,
your fears into my faith,
and your disappointments into my
hopes and dreams for you.
Amen.*

27

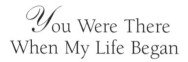

# You Were There When My Life Began

Life began
with waking up
and loving my mother's face.

*George Eliot*

*For my birth . . .*

*I thank the Lord*
*that Mom gave birth to me*
*and started me on*
*a lifelong journey*
*of loving her.*
*Amen.*

# You're My Inspiration

She's my teacher,
adviser,
and greatest inspiration.

*Whitney Houston*

*Lord, inspire me . . .*

*Through Mom's words,*
*acts of kindness,*
*gentle humility,*
*loving touch,*
*and eternal optimism that I will*
*exceed my potential*
*and overcome my self-doubts.*
*Amen.*

31

# our Shepherd

Because the Lord is my Shepherd, I have everything I need!
He lets me rest in the meadow grass and leads me
beside the quiet streams. He gives me new strength.
He helps me do what honors him the most.
Even when walking through the dark valley of death
I will not be afraid, for you are close beside me,
guarding, guiding all the way. You provide delicious
food for me in the presence of my enemies.
You have welcomed me as your guest;
blessings overflow! Your goodness and unfailing kindness
shall be with me all of my life, and afterwards
I will live with you forever in your home.

*Twenty-third Psalm, The Living Bible (TLB)*

# Lord, shepherd Mom . . .

Through all the valleys of life.
Protect her from every attack,
meet her every need,
rest and refresh her.

When she is fearful,
calm each worry
and give your strength
to endure every trial.

O God, shepherd Mom,
Carrying her gently in your arms,
that she might feel your heartbeat,
experience your breath,
and hear your voice.
Amen.

33

# Mother's Covers

When you were small
And just a touch away,
I covered you with blankets
Against the cool night air.
But now that you are tall
And out of reach,
I fold my hands
And cover you with prayer.

*Dona Maddux Cooper*

*God, answer my mother's prayers.*

*Lord,
I stand in agreement with my mother's
prayers for me, our family, and others.*

*Hear, O Lord, her every word and
heart's sigh so that all she prays might
eternally burn as a sweet incense
before your throne.
Amen.*

# *M*other's Influence

I affirm my profound belief that God's
greatest creation is womanhood.

I also believe that there is no greater
good in all the world than
motherhood.

The influence of a mother in the lives of
her children is beyond calculation.

*James E. Faust*

*God, thank you for a mother who . . .*

*Made me study.*
*Disciplined me when I needed it.*
*Praised me for a chore well done.*
*Rebuked me when I was out of line.*
*Reminded me of what was important.*
*Chastened me privately.*
*Encouraged me at just the right time.*
*Grounded me from going to the wrong places.*
*Discerned my purpose and destiny.*
*Worked incessantly on my weaknesses.*
*And above all,*
*Forgave and loved me through it all.*
*Amen.*

# $\mathcal{M}$om, My Teacher

It is not what you do for your children
but what you have taught them to do for
themselves that will make them
successful human beings.

*Ann Landers*

*Teach me, O Lord . . .*

*Important life lessons through my mom*
*that I may learn at her feet*
*the virtues of purity, honesty, and*
*patience.*

*Teach me, O Lord,*
*through my mom*
*the lessons of experience so that I*
*may benefit from her successes*
*and learn from her mistakes.*

*Thank you, O Lord,*
*that Mom's life is a textbook on how to*
*live life with courage and grace.*
*Amen.*

# $\mathcal{G}$race

A mother loves her children even when
they least deserve to be loved.

*Kate Samperi*

*For mercy and grace . . .*

*In Mom's actions and words,*
*I am forever grateful, dear Lord.*

*She extended grace to me when I hadn't*
*earned it,*
*And she showed mercy when I deserved*
*punishment and rebuke.*

*Lord, I saw your face*
*of mercy and grace*
*in Mom.*
*Thanks.*
*Amen.*

# A Mother's Secret Hope

Youth fades, love droops,
the leaves of friendship fall;
a mother's secret hope
outlives them all.

*Oliver Wendell Holmes*

# Hope

*God, enable me to return to Mom*
*the gift of hope she deposited in me.*

*Empower me to help her.*

*Inspire me to lift her spirit.*

*Release me to be there*
*when she needs me.*

*Most of all, Lord,*
*When life becomes a burden for her,*
*entrust me to carry both her and the*
*burden across the tears and lay her under*
*the shadow of thy wings.*
*Amen.*

# May the Lord Bless My Mom

May the Lord bless and protect you;

may the Lord's face radiate with joy
because of you;

may he be gracious to you,
show you his favor,
and give you his peace.

*The Aaronic Blessing*

*Bless you, Mom.*

*As you drive,*
God bless you.
*As you work,*
God bless you.
*As you cook,*
God bless you.
*As you go out and come in,*
God bless you.
*As you get up and lie down,*
God bless you.
*At all times and in every way,*
God bless you!

# *D*ear Mom

As I walk through my museum of memories,
I owe you—for your *time*. Day and night.
I owe you—for your *sacrifices*. Numerous
and quickly forgotten.
I owe you—for your *faith*. Solid and sure.
I owe you—for your *hope*. Ceaseless and
indestructible.
I owe you—for your *love*. Devoted and
deep.

*Charles R. Swindoll*

## Welcome home.

*Lord, I remember the days*
*when Mom would welcome me home.*
*She would wash and bandage my hurts.*
*She would let me clean the dough out of*
*the cookie bowl.*
*She would drive me to baseball practices*
*and insist on baths even when I didn't*
*need them.*

*Now, Lord,*
*when Mom needs help up the steps,*
*a listening ear,*
*a place to live,*
*or a hand to hold,*
*may I be the one to say to Mom,*
*"Welcome home."*
*Amen.*

# $\mathcal{M}$om, I'm Counting on You

Mother is the one we count on for the
things that matter most of all.

*Katherine Butler Hathaway*

*Count on me.*

*Lord,*
*Whisper the sweet assurance*
*into my mother's ear*
*that just as I've always counted on her,*
*she can count on me.*
*Amen.*

# Always Praying for You

*Pray without ceasing.*

*1 Thessalonians 5:17 New King James Version (NKJV)*

*Help me, Lord . . .*

To remember Mom daily in my prayers.
When I wake, to pray for her protection.
As I eat, to pray for her provision.
When I work, to pray for her labor.
As I play, to pray for her enjoyment.
When I sit, to pray for her rest.
Amen.

# *M*om's Love

Mother love is the fuel
that enables a normal human being
to do the impossible.

*Unknown*

*Mom, pray for me . . .*

*When I face the impossible,*
*When I must believe the improbable,*
*When I must push*
*through the impenetrable,*
*O God, prompt Mom to pray for me.*
*Amen.*

# Mother's Forgiveness

The heart of a mother is a deep abyss at
the bottom of which you will always
find forgiveness.

*Honoré de Balzac*

*I pray for forgiveness . . .*

Lord,
Deep within my mother's heart,
help her find the love to forgive me
for all the unkind things I've said
and mean things I've done to her.
Amen.

# *I* Honor You

Honor your father and mother,
that you may have a long, good life
in the land the Lord your God
will give you.

*The Decalogue*

*Honoring you in prayer . . .*

*Lord,*
*I pray blessings and honor on my mom.*

*Honor her in her work*
*before all her colleagues.*

*Honor her in the city*
*before all her neighbors.*

*Honor her in the home*
*before her husband and children.*

*Honor her name whenever and wherever*
*it is spoken.*
*Amen.*

# You Read to Me

You may have tangible wealth untold:
Caskets of jewels and coffers of gold.
Richer than I you can never be
I had a mother who read to me.

*Strickland Gillilan*

*For a mom who read to me . . .*

I thank you, God.

When she read the Scriptures,
I saw thy face.

When she told the old, old stories,
I heard thy voice.

When she read about signs and wonders,
I felt thy power.

How awesome it was, O God,
To hear thy word through Mom's voice.

Amen.

# *A* Hug

The story of a mother's life:

"Trapped between a scream and a hug."

*Cathy Guisewite*

*A prayer hug for you . . .*

*Across the miles,*
*Spirit of God,*
*carry a hug,*
*from me to Mom.*
*Wrap her in thy arms and hold her tight.*
*Amen.*

# Mothers

Not for the star-crowned heroes,
the men that conquer and slay,
But a song for those that bore them,
the mothers braver than they.
With never a blare of trumpets,
with never a surge of cheers,
They march to the unseen hazard—
pale, patient volunteers.

*Mark De Wolfe Howe*

*Beyond words . . .*

*Lord,
I have not the words to express
all my feelings
and thankfulness for Mom.*

*So even as you created the universe,
setting the stars and galaxies in place,
please form on my lips
the praise I would give for my mom
who gave so much to me.
Amen.*

# *M*om's Wisdom

My mother drew a distinction between
*achievement* and *success.*
She said that *achievement* is the
knowledge that you have studied and
worked hard and done the best
that is in you.
*Success* is being praised by others, and
that's nice, too,
but not as important or satisfying.
Always aim for *achievement* and forget
about *success.*

*Helen Hayes*

*I've learned so much from you.*

*Lord,*
*Help me to apply the wisdom that Mom*
*taught me that I may go far*
*beyond success in life.*

*May my mom's achievement be that she*
*has a child who*
*wholeheartedly loves thee*
*and fervently loves others.*
*Amen.*

# God's Hands

I have held many things in my hands and
lost them all;
But the things I have placed in God's
hands, those I always possess.

*Earline Steelburg*

# By the hand . . .

*God, I'm asking you to*
*Take Mom by the hand,*
*Guide her through every valley,*
*Help her climb every mountain,*
*Be her strength and*
*comfort in every trial.*

*God, I know I cannot be all that my*
*mother needs . . . but you can.*

*Please, God, take Mom by the hand.*

*Amen.*

# *U*nselfishly

You have to love your children
unselfishly.

It's hard.

But it is the only way.

*Barbara Bush*

*A mother's love . . .*

*God,*
*I learned about your love from Mother.*

*While her love was imperfect,*
*You filled in the gaps with grace*
*and the mistakes with forgiveness.*

*So, God,*
*enable me to love my children*
*with Mother's love.*

*Amen.*

# *P*lans

It's not the plan we create
That determines our fulfillment.

It's what we let God do
In the plan of his choosing.

*Galphre Gilliland*

*I pray for Mother's plans . . .*

*That each comes
from the heart of God—*

*inspired by goodness,
motivated by love,
filled with hope,
and strengthened with patient
persistence,*

*so that fulfillment of her dreams will
overflow in all of her plans.
Amen.*

71

# Today

Yesterday is gone.
Remember the good.
Learn from the bad.
Let go of the hurts.

Tomorrow has yet to arrive.
Abandon the worries.
Plan what's prudent.
Dream the impossible.

Today is all we have.
Cherish the moment.
Love others and be kind.
Do your best.
Trust God with the rest.

*Mom, I'm praying for you today.*

*Lord,*
*Setting aside procrastination and good*
*intentions,*
*I am praying now for Mother.*

*I pray for her to be in good health,*
*speak kind words,*
*cherish each moment,*
*and find love in every encounter.*

*May today be better than her yesterdays.*

*May tomorrow be filled with hope and dreams,*
*not worries and fears.*
*Amen.*

# Seek God

God only comes
to those who ask him to come;
and he cannot refuse to come
to those who implore him
long, often, and ardently.

*Simone Weil*

*I'm praying that you will seek God.*

Lord,
answer Mom's prayers.

When she seeks thee,
Hide not thy face.

When she hungers for thee,
feed her the bread of life.

When she thirsts,
satisfy her with living water.

And when she comes to thee,
gather her, I pray, into thy presence and
shelter her from every storm.
Amen.

# Refuge and Fortress

He who dwells in the shelter
of the Most High
Will abide in the shadow
of the Almighty.
I will say to the LORD, "My refuge and
my fortress,
My God, in whom I trust!"

*Psalm 91:1–2 NKJV*

*God, shelter Mom . . .*

*From crazy drivers,*
*From thieves and robbers,*
*From unkind words and acts,*
*From gossiping friends,*
*From unwise decisions,*
*From foolish desires,*
*From worldly temptations,*
*From deceitful thoughts,*
*From abuse and addiction,*
*From vicious attacks,*
*From demons and devils,*
*From all that is evil,*
*Shelter Mom under thy wings.*
*Amen.*

# Love's Garment

Love has a hem to her garment
That reaches to the very dust.
It sweeps the stains from
the streets and lanes,
and because it can,
it must.

*Mother Teresa*

*Clothe Mother with love.*

*God,*
*across the miles and years,*
*weave your love and mine,*
*into a splendid garment of beauty,*
*and clothe my mom,*
*in this garment of love,*
*so that all her days,*
*she will always know*
*she is loved.*
*Amen.*

# Love Is

Love is patient, love is kind.
It does not envy,
it does not boast,
it is not proud.
It is not rude,
it is not self-seeking,
it is not easily angered,
it keeps no record of wrongs.
Love does not delight in evil
but rejoices with the truth.
Love always protects, always trusts,
always hopes, always perseveres.
Love never fails.

*Corinthians 13:4–8 New International Version (NIV)*

*With love, I'm praying for you, Mom.*

*God,*
*How I love my mother!*
*With every word and act,*
*Help me show Mom I love her.*

*May my every prayer for Mom*
*be a loving embrace*
*that crowns her days*
*with joy and peace.*

*Amen.*

## Acknowledgments

My deepest thanks to Patty, Lillian, and all the supportive people at Andrews McMeel Universal who helped make this book a reality. Special thanks to Lois, who believed in this project, and to my closest friend and loving mother to our three children, Judi.